[an important no

hello.

hello to my unhealed, to my mentally unwell, to my readers wondering when it will get easier.

i am so sorry we had to find each other in this way, that we met across pages of unhappy healing rather than descriptions of our joys for living, but know that we will bond in our brokenness.

know that we were not born this way, with baby's gums whispering of sadness or trembling hands. if we were whole once before, we can be once again. i promise you that.

this is your book as much as it is mine, so use it. scribble on every page, write your own poems in retaliation- hell, burn it if you have to. just use it. do something with it. heal with it.

as always, i'll use no capital letters, *except on a few odd occasions*. these are the pages and the phrases i really want you to play the closest attention to. remember these sentences, reread them a few times, relax into the words until you feel comforted.

this book contains many poems that talk of triggering subjects. suicidal thoughts, self harm, depression, substance abuse and severe mental health are topics mentions throughout. please guard your heart and only read this book when you feel safe enough to do so. your wellbeing is so important. these poems are not going anywhere, they can wait patiently for you to read them.

i love you, my sunflowers.
bloom with me again.

1

[contents.]

pg 5 ....losing yourself.

pg 28 ....letting go.

pg 43 ....learning to heal.

pg 72 ....love living again.

pg 101 ....a goodbye.

pg 102 ....acknowledgements.

how to be mentally well.

[and stay that way.]

illustrations by amber mia paul
isbn 978-1-7391789-1-8

this book is dedicated to:

the people who have held me up.
my mother,
my friends
and at times,
myself.

i am indebted to you all.

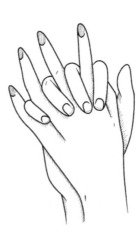

losing yourself

[because it's hard not to nowadays.]

how to be mentally well

most mornings,
i wake up
and beg to fall back asleep.

i beg for closed curtains
and dark rooms.

i beg for heavy blankets
and quiet comforts.

i beg for forgiveness.
from myself,
from the world,
from the morning.

i beg for self love
and kindness
and warm arms.

i beg and beg and beg
and my pleads fall on my own deaf ears
in my own empty room
on a stupid,
stupid morning.

so i just fall back asleep.

[what do you beg for?]

....
....
....
....
....
....
....
....
....
....
....
....
....
....
....
....
....
....
....
....
....
....
....

how to be mentally well

there must be only so many times
that i can plead with myself for
kindness.

i can't keep begging for this.

how to be mentally well

i can't seem to stop hurting myself.
i'm killing myself with
cigarettes and
boys and
vodka and
driving too fast and
not eating enough and
my hair is falling out and
my face is so pale and
i am longing to see the sun again.

i'm dying.

i make out that i do not know
what to do to stop it,
because it is far easier than admitting:

i
just
don't
want
to.

i do not have the energy,
or the willingness,
for recovery.

how to be mentally well

do i look as *soft* as my heart feels?

how to be mentally well

[a journal entry from november 22nd 2021.]

*i am tearing myself apart. i am causing myself so.
much. pain. i really wish i was kinder to me. and i can
see it happening too. it's like some fucked up train
wreck that you can't take your eyes off. you know it's
going to end badly and with a hell of a lot of hurt for
everyone involved but you can't. look. away.*

*i'm the train __and__ the train-tracks __and__ the conductor
__and__ the bystander watching.*

this is going to end badly for me.

__*i know it.*__

how to be mentally well

[a journal entry from ....]

....
....
....
....
....
....
....
....
....
....
....
....
....
....
....
....
....
....
....
....
....
....
....
....

how to be mentally well

i don't write *'good'* poetry,
unless i am destroyed.

i must be sat on my kitchen floor,
cross legged,
with streaked cheeks and tear stained t-shirt's.

i must be starving
from three days of neglected hunger
and three years of neglected recovery.

i must be sleep deprived
and romance deprived
and kindness deprived
and happiness deprived.

i have to be
absolutely
broken.

and to be honest, this poem is shit.

because by some ironically funny, cosmic chance
i seem to be doing somewhat okay today.
and for some reason,
for some sick, twisted, fucked up reason,
that makes me feel
far too broken to write about.

how to be mentally well

[draw what's going on inside of your head.]

how to be mentally well

for just once,
i wanted someone other than myself,
to notice
that i was becoming a shell of myself.

how to be mentally well

i don't want to tell you about how i harm myself.
i know you'll look at me funny,
with pity and a tilted head
like i'm damaged goods.

i don't want to tell you how i burn myself on days
where the world feels a little too cold,
where the heat is the only thing that makes me
feel something.

i don't want to tell you about how i abuse my heart,
how i let bad men break it,
in the hopes i will ruin
a few more pieces of myself.

i don't want to tell you about how i drink
disgusting amounts
to forget what my body looks like,
it is easier to shower when i cannot feel my own hands.

i don't want to tell you *any of this*
but i cannot seem to stop myself.

how to be mentally well

i cannot look myself in the eyes for much longer.
my vision is blurring and
my hands are shaking
and my mind is missing
everything that i used to be.

i remember when i was happy.
i miss that.

how to be mentally well

i want to return home.
<u>i want to belong to a home again.</u>

and if home is not a place,
but the feeling of upmost happiness and belonging,
then,
since i do not ever feel like i *truly belong*,
i suppose you could label me as homeless.

perhaps,
in the way that a bird who cannot fly will
eventually return to the earth,

and a tree
who's roots are too intertwined with another,
fighting for the right to exist,
will lose its greenness,

perhaps i will fade into nothing without my home.

how to be mentally well

and we wonder why humans have such a need of
belonging.

[what does belonging mean to you?]

....
....
....
....
....
....
....
....
....
....
....
....
....
....
....
....
....
....
....
....
....
....
....
....
....

my mental health
is suffocating
me.
it has swept
me up in
its storm
and no one
can see
me gasping for
breath.

or-

if they *can*
see,
they have
turned around
and are
pretending
not to.

how to be mentally well

i think i may to die soon.

metaphorically speaking, i think i already have, i'm just waiting for my body to catch up with my mind. i know i can't carry on like this any longer and i feel so damn weak admitting it but i can't do it.

i just can't do it anymore.

how to be mentally well

[a journal entry from ....]

....
....
....
....
....
....
....
....
....
....
....
....
....
....
....
....
....
....
....
....
....
....
....
....

how to be mentally well

i don't know who i am anymore.
i don't recognise myself in the mirror
or perceive my body as mine when i touch it.

i've lost touch with myself,
i've disconnected my mind with my body.

i want to know myself again.

i want to hold my body as mine again
and feel my skin as my own.

let me enjoy living again. please.
let me enjoy my favourite foods
and my favourite people
and my favourite places.

i miss how healthy
happiness used to taste.

how to be mentally well

I WANT TO RELEARN WHO I AM.

letting go

[of everything you cannot control,
even if you wish you could.]

how to be mentally well

i was taught to hate myself,

to envy the girls that are
everything
i am not.

i was made to destroy every tiny slither
of self love
i could have ever held.

i was alone and in pieces and broken.
and i know
it's going to take months,
before i'll even be able look in a mirror again,
without sobbing,
or pulling at my skin.

i have been utterly consumed
by a hatred projected onto me.
by a hatred taught to me
by a hatred i was made to hold for myself.

i refuse to hate myself for any longer.

how to be mentally well

you cannot be everything and nothing all at once.

you cannot be both 'the broken'
and
'the rebuilder of others',
[even if you wish you could.]

sometimes, you just have to put yourself first.
you have to focus on rebuilding you.

how to be mentally well

[here's some space for some sad poetry.]

....
....
....
....
....
....
....
....
....
....
....
....
....
....
....
....
....
....
....
....
....
....
....
....

how to be mentally well

I CANNOT CONTAIN
WHAT IS OUT OF MY CONTROL
INTO NEAT LITTLE BOXES.

how to be mentally well

[a journal entry from december 16th 2021.]

*it's the only way i can escape living, escape my
heartbreak, escape my body. when i'm drinking, when
i'm kissing strangers, when the real world becomes
fuzzy at the edges, i can convince myself i'm okay
again. i can pretend i'm happy. i can tell myself that
when i leave this club, the cold air of the 2am winter
night won't turn me back into a shell of myself.*

*i can pretend someone is waiting up for me back home,
that someone loves me enough to make sure i get home
safe, that they want to tuck me into bed with a glass of
water for me to wake up to.*

*i can dance until my feet feel as numb as my heart does
and i can drink until my insides feel alive again.*

*it's so ugly.
i'm so sick of it.
i refuse to keep living like this.*

how to be mentally well

[a journal entry from ……………………………..]

……………………………………………………………………
……………………………………………………………………
……………………………………………………………………
……………………………………………………………………
……………………………………………………………………
……………………………………………………………………
……………………………………………………………………
……………………………………………………………………
……………………………………………………………………
……………………………………………………………………
……………………………………………………………………
……………………………………………………………………
……………………………………………………………………
……………………………………………………………………
……………………………………………………………………
……………………………………………………………………
……………………………………………………………………
……………………………………………………………………
……………………………………………………………………
……………………………………………………………………
……………………………………………………………………
……………………………………………………………………
……………………………………………………………………

life has never felt this sour before.

how to be mentally well

[what i wish someone had said to me, *but no one did so i will say it to you.*]

i know you're not doing very well right now, my love. i can see it. i can see it in the way that you act and the way that you talk and i can see it in the way that you don't. i can see it in the way you shut yourself away from the world.

i want you to know that i'm here for you. always. as you have for me, i will do anything you need me to, anything i can possibly do, to make sure you are okay again.

how to be mentally well

i want to get better,
i really do,
i'm just not sure how too.

most days,
i just feel too far gone,
like i am beyond help
like i should be labelled a lost cause.

i do want to get better.
i promise i do,

i just
don't
know
how
to.

how to be mentally well

[a journal entry from january 3rd 2022.]

i'd love to say i'm going to therapy for me, that i'm trying to heal for my own good, but honestly i think i'm doing it for everybody else.

i'm kind of a shitty person.

i sort of feel sorry for the people in my life who knew me before i became like this. i could blame it on the medication, or the trauma, but i can't keep using mental health as an excuse to push everyone away.

how to be mentally well

[a journal entry from ....]

....

....

....

....

....

....

....

....

....

....

....

....

....

....

....

....

....

....

....

....

....

....

....

....

....

how to be mentally well

if today has not been easy,
if today has left you with a withering body
and thoughts that are far less than healthy,
know that you have not failed.

let go of today.
let your hair grace your pillow case
and your mind empty onto the cotton.

today is not definitive.
it is not the
'be all and end all.'

today is just for today.

how to be mentally well

there is always
a *tomorrow*.

because there *is* always a tomorrow.

there is always another sunrise and another sunset and then another after that. there is always a new day to see and a new year to complete. there are new faces to memorise and to love and to hold carefully. there are new puddles to step in and new piles of leaves to kick. there is a never-ending rebirth of this world to witness.

and how amazing is that?

we are welcomed by this earth to witness her re-shedding again and again and again. we watch her create new life *and* mend old. our eyes are held open with curiosity and she shows us the beauty in recovery.

my darling, scream it with me:

THERE IS ALWAYS A TOMORROW.

always.
so make sure you wake up to see it.

how to be mentally well

learning to heal

[because why else are we here?]

becoming *healed* does not happen overnight,
even when we wish it would.

please do not read this chapter once and expect
to be whole again.

this is your journey.
this book is a mere pit stop.
it has a pretty view, sure,
but don't get too caught up here.
keep moving along.

keep healing.

how to be mentally well

SOMETIMES,
THINGS HAVE TO GET A LITTLE WORSE BEFORE
THEY CAN GET BETTER.

how to be mentally well

[reasons to keep going.]

- you've never seen truly how beautiful you look with wind flushed cheeks.
- each sunset is prettier than the last and you are yet to see the best one.
- coffee on cold mornings when your hands are desperate for warmth.
- the light in their eyes when you walk into the room.
- all the forehead kisses you are yet to receive.
- you are going to look amazing in next summers new clothing trends.
- and that goes for every summer that follows too.
- there are so many dogs waiting for you to scratch their heads.
- freshly washed cotton bedding.
- the smell of new books.
- holding hands and tracing palms.
- how your heart will feel when you realise you've healed the younger you.
- delicious, guilt-free desserts are just waiting patiently to be eaten by you.
- and next years birthday cake is too good to miss out on.
- peppermint tea in winter.
- your reflection is in dire need of hearing some kindness.

how to be mentally well

[your reasons to keep going:]

- ....
- ....
- ....
- ....
- ....
- ....
- ....
- ....
- ....
- ....
- ....
- ....
- ....
- ....
- ....
- ....
- ....
- ....
- ....
- ....

there is so much of the world waiting to be seen by you,
so explore it.

and if that isn't enough of a reason to keep on living,
let the thought

that the universe has corners,
existing sadly
due to not seeing your eyes,
be enough to keep going.

how to be mentally well

[a journal entry from july 22nd 2022.]

oh it's really hard, this getting better nonsense. it fucking sucks. like, <u>seriously.</u>

i think the worst part is knowing just how badly i want to get better and knowing that it's not as quick of a process as i would like. my therapist says this is normal, that everyone wishes their mental illness could be healed from immediately but she says <u>i have to be patient.</u>

apparently, recovery only works long term if you actually put some work into it. how annoying.

i am going to try though. i'm going to try really fucking hard. for my mum, for my friends and for me too. i want to get better for me. <u>i want to be happy again.</u>

how to be mentally well

[a journal entry from ....]

....
....
....
....
....
....
....
....
....
....
....
....
....
....
....
....
....
....
....
....
....
....
....
....
....
....

how to be mentally well

it is okay if healing hurts.
it is okay if it feels like your heart is being bandaged.
it is,
you just have to wait for the scarring to settle.

how to be mentally well

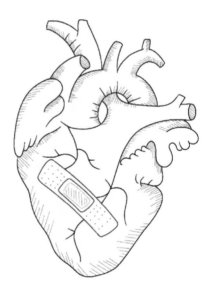

how to be mentally well

so,
while you're waiting,
you *may as well* pass the time
with some boring,
mundane fun.

[your new checklist.]

O write down a list of everything you love about yourself. trust me, there is <u>a hell of a lot</u> to love.

O go stargazing alone. be comfortable in your own silence.

O go for a walk.

O had a bed day. don't feel guilty about it.

O have another.

O read an entire book, crosslegged, sat in the sunshine [that isn't this one].

O buy some really nice tea, or coffee, or whatever it is you like to drink. enjoy it. drink slowly.

O cry in front of someone else [it really isn't weak].

O go outside and people watch. create stories about each interesting person you see.

O blare music as loud as your eardrums can take and dance around your bedroom like nobody is watching. be free.

O watch a thunderstorm. [safely.]

O write some poetry, or journal, or word vomit in your noted app, *just write something.*

O and then burn it. let go of those words as they burn into nothing. let yourself un-feel it all.

O and then write some more.

how to be mentally well

[what else do you want to put on your list?]

O ....
O ....
O ....
O ....
O ....
O ....
O ....
O ....
O ....
O ....
O ....
O ....
O ....
O ....
O ....
O ....

how to be mentally well

you _will_ find your way back to yourself.

it may just take you a while.

how to be mentally well

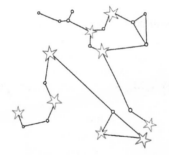

how to be mentally well

and in-case you are also trying to heal from the damage
someone else has caused,
i must remind you:

you cannot scream at someone
who just
does not
want to listen.
they will just walk away from you.

sometimes,
it's okay
to just

HEAL SILENTLY.

how to be mentally well

'heal alone,
in the middle of the night,
with a pillow case wet enough to rival the ocean.

heal in the dark,
with the curtains drawn and
the lamps switched off.

heal without sound,
with a mouth full of silence and a mind
too empty to think straight.

heal like a good victim.
don't kick up too much fuss.
don't draw attention to your traumas.

heal in private.'

<u>no.</u>
<u>fuck that.</u>

heal in public,
unashamed.

heal in the middle of the day
while you sit in the sunlight
and drink in the warmth.

heal like the good person that you are,
because you are so much more than just victim.
kick up as much fuss as you would like.
scream about it.

heal in full show.
heal without hiding yourself.
<u>god knows you've done that for long enough already.</u>

how to be mentally well

heal loudly.
heal unapologetically.
heal with friends.
heal with lovers.
heal however the fuck you'd like.

how to be mentally well

[a journal entry from august 2nd 2022.]

*i just want someone to be proud of me. i want someone
to hold me as say:*

> *'it's okay, my darling, you're doing okay.'*

*i am desperate for some sort of conformation that i am
actually getting better. i am in the presence of my mind
too often to see my changes. i just want someone to tell
me they have seen the changes.*

is that so much to ask?
does no one see me <u>that intrinsically?</u>

how to be mentally well

[a journal entry from ....]

....
....
....
....
....
....
....
....
....
....
....
....
....
....
....
....
....
....
....
....
....
....
....
....
....
....

how to be mentally well

you do not need someone else to love you before you
choose to love yourself,
but i can understand why it helps.

how to be mentally well

love me *at my worst.*

love me with my clenched fists
and my wet pillowcases.

love me with my personified heart
and transcribed tears.

love me before my legs give out
and my mind follows.

please.

love me tenderly
and with caution.

i will get better, i promise i will.

but i *need* you to love me.

how to be mentally well

[write your own version:]

love me *at my worst.*

> *love me* with my ....
> and my ....
>
> *love me* with my ....
> and my ....
>
> *love me* with my ....
> and my ....

please.

> *love me* ....
> ....

i will get better, i promise i will.

but i *need* you to love me.

being loved while mentally unwell is really, *really* hard. it's shitty and confusing and unbelievably difficult. not just for you, but for them.

sometimes it feels like you're stuck in this cycle of begging for love and refusing it out of blatant stubbornness. most mornings, you'll wake up and despise the idea of somebody desiring you and most evenings, you'll cocoon yourself around whichever warm body will let you for the night. there's just something about nighttimes that leave us so vulnerably alone.

i can't tell you how to resolve this, i wish i could, but there's no one quick fix to loving with mental illness.

it takes time to navigate. it takes a while to explain to someone how you need both space and closeness. it takes carefulness to describe how you need to be loved.

you can do it, though. you can be loved and still learning to love yourself.

IT JUST TAKES SOME PATIENCE.

[*if* you want to be loved, *how* do you want to be loved?]

....
....
....
....
....
....
....
....
....
....
....
....
....
....
....
....
....
....
....
....
....
....
....
....
....

how to be mentally well

i have come to understand
that even though i feel *absolutely broken,*
it does not mean that i am.

i can still be a whole person with mental illness,

i am still a person
who deserves love
and wants kindness.

i am more than worthy of gentle hands
and fingers that don't prod
at my scars.

kiss me on the tip of my nose
before you press our foreheads together
so that i may share the love you give me
between our touching faces.

show me that i can be loved regardless.

how to be mentally well

i would like to remind you,
though,
that you do not need another's love to love yourself.

remember:

SELF-LOVE IS ENOUGH.

how to be mentally well

i may always be alone,
but that does not mean i am destined
to be lonely.
if i can find comfort in my own company,
i know
i will be happy
regardless,

even if i only have me
to love me.

how to be mentally well

you must learn to hold your own heart kindly
and softly.
she is fragile,
she is forgiving
and she is slightly needy *at the best of times.*

BE KIND TO YOUR BODY.

love living again

[you deserve nothing less than pure happiness.]

how to be mentally well

sometimes,
on mornings
where i cannot even think about opening my curtains
[because the thought of sunlight gives me a headache],
i sit cross legged in my bed
and hold my heart in my hands.

i am tender with her,
gentle and soft.

i find comfort in hearing her beat,
knowing how i hold so much power in my body.

i feel like i have died
over and over and over

and yet,
here i am.
in my warm bed,
still coping.

still alive.

and then i get up,
open the curtains
[but the sunlight can't actually hurt me],
and i let the sun see my teeth for once.
i smile at the world and at my heart in my hands
and i say to myself:

'TODAY IS GOING TO BE OKAY AGAIN.'

how to be mentally well

[incase no one has told you this today:]

i hope you know how much i love you,
how much you mean to me.

you're my world.

you,
genuinely,
are the only thing i care about.

i adore you.

how to be mentally well

i will be happy again.
i promise myself,
i promise i will be.
i will work on it.
hard.
i will love me.
i am enough.

how to be mentally well

[your daily affirmations. speak it into existence.]

- ....
- ....
- ....
- ....
- ....
- ....
- ....
- ....
- ....
- ....
- ....
- ....
- ....
- ....
- ....
- ....
- ....
- ....
- ....
- ....
- ....
- ....
- ....
- ....

how to be mentally well

YOU DESERVE TO LOVE YOURSELF,
MENTAL ILLNESS AND ALL.

how to be mentally well

[draw what's going on inside of your head *now*.]

how to be mentally well

[my favourite butterfly effects.]

secretly smoking my first
cigarette on a school trip
at 14 on a teachers
balcony > living with
15 strangers in the middle
of nowhere.

moving to spain
for 2 months to live
with my [then]
boyfriend > becoming
a poet.

breaking my wrist figure skating
at 8 > organising all the parties
for the basketball team
at the university
of my dreams.

downloading tinder > my burning house tattoo.

lying about an imaginary
birthday party > sending
love letters back
and forth with an artist.

how to be mentally well

[your favourite butterfly effects.]

....

....

....

....

....

....

....

....

....

....

....

....

....

....

....

....

how to be mentally well

· ·
· ·
· ·
· ·

· ·
· ·
· ·
· ·

· ·
· ·
· ·
· ·

· ·
· ·
· ·
· ·

now,
i think its about time for some soppy, self-love poetry,
don't you?

for a *good while*,
i had thought recovering from my mental illness
would be the end of the *'me'* that i knew.

i'd existed with *it* for so long,
i didn't know how to be me
<u>without</u> my mental illness.

but now-
now that i've seen
and felt
what it's like
to live without *it* holding me back,

i don't *want* to live any other way.

<u>I LOVE THE HEALED ME.</u>

how to be mentally well

i think i must be lucky to be here,
living the life that i am.

it is nothing exceptional,
it is nothing out of a movie,
it is nothing short of average,

but it is mine.
and i love it.

how to be mentally well

you are destined
to love kind people,

to see sunlight in the mornings,
to feel the grass between your toes.

you are made for this,
i promise you.

allow your heart to climb up into your head
and stay there.

do not pick between the two of them
ever again.

live furiously
and experience mundanity ferociously.

the world is yours for the taking.

how to be mentally well

i hope to never write
an unhappy poem
ever
again.

i hope to let my wrists
feel the warmth of my jumpers sleeves
and the
softness of the people i let touch me.

i hope to grace my eyes
with the faces of those
who i long to
carefully hold.

i hope to touch palms
not only in romance,
and not only
with another undressed body.

i hope to speak words of kindness
even when my throat
is begging
for unpleasantness.

i hope to be content,
even on the days
that are far less
than ideal.

how to be mentally well

i hope to cope with sadness
healthily
and without
an impending sense of doom.

                              i hope to love living.
                                    every hour,
                                    of every day,
            of every month that i am lucky enough to see.

i hope to shake myself to the core
every time i look in the mirror
and am shocked by
the beauty staring back at me.

                              i hope to fill pages
                                    and pages
                                    and pages
                              with my happiness.

i hope to never write
an unhappy poem
ever
again.

                    [but if i do,
        if, by chance, this is not the end of my healing
              i will know that i have healed before.
            i am more than capable of doing it again.]

[what do you hope for?]

....

....

....

....

        ....

        ....

        ....

        ....

....

....

....

....

        ....

        ....

        ....

        ....

how to be mentally well

....
....
....
....

          ....
          ....
          ....
          ....

....
....
....
....

          ....
          ....
          ....
          ....

how to be mentally well

IT IS A PLEASURE TO LIVE IN THIS BODY.

how to be mentally well

i could go on <u>forever.</u>

i could write you thousands of poems detailing
how brilliant it feels to be healed,
but i would rather
you feel it for yourself.
i would rather
you write it for yourself.

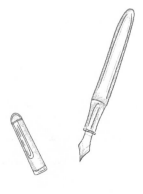

[tell me about how great it feels to be happy again.]

....
....
....
....
....
....
....
....
....
....
....
....
....
....
....
....
....
....
....
....
....
....
....
....

how to be mentally well

[a journal entry from september 5th 2022.]

for once, i think i'm really, truly happy.

i think i've done it.

i'm not saying this is going to last forever, but god right now i am so enjoying being me. and it feels so alien. i'm not used to waking up to mirrors that aren't covered in bedsheet, or drinking socially for fun without taking it too far but i like who i'm becoming.

i really, really do.

how to be mentally well

[a journal entry from ....]

....
....
....
....
....
....
....
....
....
....
....
....
....
....
....
....
....
....
....
....
....
....
....
....
....
....
....
....

if you have made it this far and you still feel like you are stuck on chapter one or chapter two or even chapter three, *you have not failed.*

like i said, this book is as much yours as it is mine. it is yours to heal from. you may need to spend some extra time on some chapters and you may not come back to this last one for months, maybe even years. this is okay. this is normal. this is healing.

be patient.

*GOOD THINGS REALLY DO COME TO THOSE
WHO WAIT.*

how to be mentally well

how to be mentally well

please do not rush to read the ending of this book.

as cliché as it feels,
this is one book
you truly cannot skip
straight to the end of.

you *have* to heal at your own pace.

now that you're nearing the end
of our journey together,

i do have a little favour to ask.

.

how to be mentally well

i want you to reread this book.

i want you to marvel at your doodles and the
collections of words that *you* have strung together.

i want you to look at how *you* have processed your
emotions, look at how far *you* have come, look at how
you have bloomed.

i want you to know that you are wonderful. i mean it.

you should be so proud of yourself, of the journey you
have been on. you have metaphorically climbed
mountains and swam rivers and scaled cliff faces. you
have achieved a hell of a lot and i am so grateful to
have been with you while you have done it.

even if we only meet across these pages, with me in
your palms and my words in your mind, it is plenty for
me. i am so lucky to share this space with you.

reread this book and acknowledge your growth, your
newfound self-love, your beautiful journey.

we both know that this is not the 'be all and end all' of
recovery, but treat this book as a transcribed healing.

how to be mentally well

life *will* go on.
we *will* be okay.

i can feel it in my bones.

[a goodbye.]

i hope you can close this book with the knowledge that
you are worth every second of recovery. please
understand that i have meant every word of this book,
of the conversation we have had across these pages.

please take care of yourself.

until the next time you need me, my love. perhaps we
will find each other again between these poems,
between the self-love and the healing.

i will be here,
just in case,
waiting for whenever you need me.

goodbye,
my sunflowers.

[acknowledgements.]

i didn't know it was possible to fall *more* in love with
poetry, but time and time again i am proven wrong.
writing this book was one of the most healing things i
have ever done and i thank you for the opportunity to
do that.

thank you to my readers. thank you to the people who
have broken our hearts. thank you to the people who
put us back together.

thank you to my support systems; my friends, my
family, my loved ones. thank you for always believing
in me, for always being there for me. i am in debt to
you all.

thank you to myself. i am so grateful to be me. i love
the shattered parts of myself and the wonky,
glued-back-together pieces that shine under moonlight.
i am thankful for how i healed myself.

thank you for anyone who has ever watched my tiktoks,
or read my work. i love you all endlessly and i will
forever thank you for the chance to keep writing. you
have made me the happiest version of myself i could
have ever hoped to be.

thank you.
thankyouthankyouthankyou.

[other books by isabella dorta.]

- 'how sunflowers bloom under moonlight'
  [available on amazon.]

- 'how to be mentally well'
  [available on amazon.]

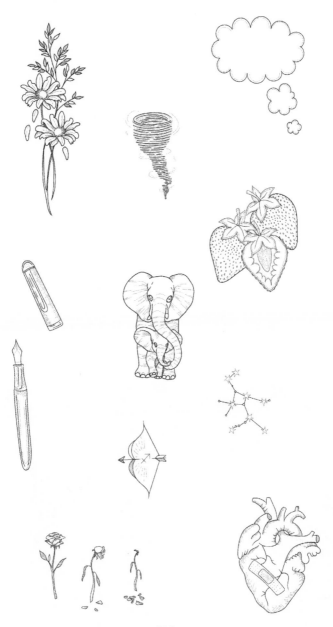

Printed in the USA
CPSIA information can be obtained
at www.ICGtesting.com
LVHW041427200923
758798LV00004B/149